Dedicated To:

Our wonderful granddaughter, Lucy Ann, and her caring and loving parents. May this wonderful child, and every other child, be given the opportunity to realize their full potential. America, and every other country, owes this to their most precious assets.

Once upon a time, now that is a good start and even a fractured fairy tale will emerge, there was a retired couple, with three lovely, compassionate, and professionally established daughters, comfortably enjoying their lives, and even at times tasting the wine and smelling the roses. And while in this retired lifestyle, there came a wonderful gift of joy, the soon to be child of our youngest daughter and her companion. Me-Maw and Pop-Pop joyfully awaited Lucy Ann's birth, a blessing for sure, but stressful for a forty-year-old mother, resulting in a Caesarian delivery and a bout of post preeclampsia. Nonetheless the parents managed this with amazing strength, love, and devotion to their newborn. Me-Maw & Pop-Pop also helped a little. The parents provided a caring and healthy environment for their little bundle of joy, their Lucy Ann, and from the very first day started reading stories to her. Lucy Ann's parents have continued to immerse her in the world of books and reading, and even have taught her to laugh a little.

Lucy certainly has her moments, but Lucy's stressful moments return to laughing and engaging with others, with of course, diversionary tactics by parents, and grandparents. Lucy loves to have stories read to her and will often just page through the books and relive the stories in her own mind. Her parents also devoted effort to sleep habits and eating a variety of healthy foods. All these efforts have served Lucy Ann well as she enters her fourth year of life. It is those simple, free, and beautiful things in life, parents, and grandparents, need as their everyday companions.

The birth of a child, life's wonderful joy, is the essence of life and the embodiment of all that is creative. The magnificence of the human body's design, certainly a manifestation of a being greater than the sum of all that we know, or will ever know, allows the joining of two to create a third. The event is the most spiritual and most uplifting feeling one can have. The experience of seeing the exit of this creation from the woman's womb is the most miraculous, mind altering, and life-long memory two people can have. This birth is a blessing, not only to the parents and supporting family members, but to the world at large. Procreation is the lifeblood of human existence and when a child is born it is not only the parents joy and responsibility to nurture the growth of the child through childhood and adolescence, toward responsible adulthood, but it is everyone's responsibility to do everything possible to aid and insure this happens.

Societies can enhance the human condition, if everyone, supported, and insisted on, policies that treated *"Every Child is Everyone's Child,"* providing early and equal education, sustainable family incomes, and a sense of dignity and hope for all. And yes, these policies have a cost to them, but the cost of not adhering to this concept is far greater in terms of broken homes, drug addiction, crime, unnecessary incarcerations, and wasted talent.

The One, greater than all that we are, has created this magnificent process of birth, it is for all to do a better job of respecting, supporting, and enjoying this process. Humanity is free to accept the concept of

"Every Child is Everyone's Child," it is simple and beautiful, and the human experience's best companion.

And now back to the fractured fairy-tale. Me-Maw and Pop-Pop, from the very moment of birth, dedicated themselves to doing everything within their means to help with the nurturing of this special gift in our lives. And from that moment the parents immersed themselves in the loving care and nurturing of their precious creation. The effort of course depletes one's energy reservoir, but the sheer joy of holding this creation in one's arms, watching their eyes wander, their tiny hands grip your fingers with unimaginable strength, and just wondering what is going on in that early brain, makes the depletion seem to evaporate in the air. For the first two years of Lucy's life, Me- Maw, and Pop-Pop participated two days a week to help with the care of this child. Feeding formula, and breast- pumped mother's milk, changing diapers, doing laundry, house cleaning, rocking of course and reading stories, were all part of the routine, exhausting for two seniors, but the joy of caring for her absorbed the weariness of those monotonous tasks. To watch this child grow is a magnificent adventure, laden with all sorts of surprises, but one that is worthy of our time and effort.

It was always fascinating to experience the next progression in the child's development, from the first sign of crawling, the utterance of the first words, (hopefully Me-Maw or Pop-Pop; somewhat of a stretch), the first steps (Accidental tourist for sure), the ingestion of solid food (Oh no she is going to choke), developing eating skills (dexterity at its best), the use of a napkin (unreal), the progressions are endless, simple and beautiful to experience. The magnificence of the human creation, with all its intricacies and complexities, is surely an overwhelming experience. The movement of those little fingers, one of the body's mechanisms that is undaunting in its majestic design, is a wonderment to watch. That little grip around our fingers calls out a bonding that is magical in its simplicity, but certainly complex in its mechanics. Does the child gain a sense of comfort from this action, a means of bonding while its relational senses are developing?

Magical for sure. These moments are cherished and remembered for a lifetime. All should indulge in these precious moments, to the benefit of all. Me-Maw and Pop-Pop have done just that with amazing warmth and joy.

Those early years of life are so important, it seems, to the healthy development of the child, and ones that may determine the success and moral development throughout that child's lifetime. Early years of reading to the child and the saturation of their developing minds with wonderful fairy tales, children's fantasies, adorable animals, baby-sitting grandparents, dinosaurs, witches, the heavens above, the oceans below and even monsters, are great investments with enormous returns. Endless to be sure, but so enriching for those little but cherished minds. Lucy Ann, even at her earliest moments on this earth, would attempt to bond when Me-Maw or Pop-Pop held her in their arms and read a story to her. Just the sound of voices, and the warmth of our touch, penetrating her yet limited world, must establish a comforting universe for this developing wonder, one that establishes an element of security that may last throughout their lives. Fascinating to witness the development of the child's mind as parents, and grandparents, continue to read throughout those early years, for it was enlightening to hear Lucy Ann, when able to speak but not yet actually reading, to narrate the story from memory when Me-Maw or Pop-Pop would miss a sentence, or worst yet a whole page. Yes, Me-Maw's and Pop- Pop's do make mistakes, reading stories over and over do become tedious at times for the best of us, but it is a just reward to hear that replay and correction from that wonderfully developing mind.

The expansion of their imagination, and understanding of the universe around them, increases with that early reading. The magnitude of the expansion is not important, but the fact that it appears to expand is. Wonder and joy to experience this.

And the endless diaper changes in those early years, carefully wiping that tender bottom, flushing the remains, and encountering that youthful resistance with accompanying vocals, was always a challenge for Me-Maw and Pop-Pop, but also produced tender moments.

Attempting to hold down a squiggling, vocalizing child, while removing the diaper and imploring the heavens to minimize any further mess required a tag-team effort by Me-Maw and Pop-Pop. What is going on in that little one's mind as two people try to wrap something around their little derriere? Is it slight trauma for the young child, as the child is exposed to this new experience? Fortunately, Me-Maw, with years of experience with three little ones, implored a technique of mimicking the vocalizing child with her own renditions of discomfort, and transformed the child into a tranquil and laughing wonder. Lucy Ann always seemed to respond well to those interacting with her as her view of the new world unfolded before her. It was as if the child responded well to an effort to understand the turmoil or chaos within her unfolding view of her new life. Me-Maw's mimicking technique, off-key singing (Lucy in the Sky with Diamonds, a favorite), and even a few tickles, "Tikey Wickeys" in Pop-Pop vernacular, always brought a calming and humorous end to what could be a messy event. The dexterity of that young child on a dressing table is frightening at times, with a slip here or there, but it is a testament to the magnificence of the human creation in all its glory. Does the child's transition from that cozy and self-sustaining comfortable womb of the mother to the unending and dependent experiences of its new life get our most compassionate response? Always something new and something to learn as its world unfolds. Something parents, grandparents and society must ensure that there is always a compassionate response. It is frustrating not to be able to understand fully the meanderings and developing perspectives of that expanding young mind, but it is a challenge, and a joy, to use all our efforts to engage with it. And yes, even deceitful techniques employed by Grandparents are acceptable in taking control of all early situations.

The progression of Lucy Ann's eating skills was an engaging experience to say the least with Me-Maw and Pop-Pop quickly learning to deflect the impromptu food projectiles launched from the little princess's food bunker.

Messy to us but appeared to bring boundless joy to the little devil within. It was great sport to try to place the spoonful of solid food within Lucy Ann's mouth, without spraying Me-Maw or Pop-Pop, with that meal's food offering. It surely was a sport of sorts for Lucy Ann, mixing the intake of nourishment with registering a showering culinary protest, and a violation of her physical space, without prior approval. What goes on in that child's mind-space, when the child experiences new things in their expanding world? It is mind boggling to imagine what is going on in that new mind, when not too long ago, within that comfortable womb, the child's sustenance came from an attached cord, and no big fuss to feeding. A world of difference to be sure. Messy, but always a joy and a few laughs, sitting at the table with Lucy Ann securely in her food bunker. Lucy Ann had this technique, Pop-Pop named it the "side-head," of flopping her head, to one side or the other, to prevent food from entering her sacred cavity.

Defensive in nature, but a true artform to behold, the little one's creative response to her unfolding world. Me- Maw and Pop-Pop, of course, had developed tactics to mitigate Lucy Ann's antics. Me-Maw did her mimicking "side-head" flops with swirling hair affects and Pop-Pop had his spidery hand movement across the table to regain Lucy Ann's full attention. A little laughter, a little eating was the essence of our table etiquette with Lucy Ann.

Amusing at times too, watching Lucy Ann yearning to mimic our behavior by wanting the same type of napkin, fork, or glass that Me-Maw or Pop-Pop were using. Always a proud moment in Lucy Ann's life, I believe, when she dined as everyone else did.

A defining moment in Lucy Ann's culinary development was when Pop- Pop decided to make Linguine with Clam sauce one night and Lucy Ann appeared interested in trying what Me- Maw and Pop-Pop were eating. Well, from the first inhale of those long pasta strands, emerged, from that day forward, a pasta queen unmatched in veracity and allegiance to the Italian cuisine. All these table encounters were a bit messy, but Me-Maw had a creative technique of cleaning up the little princess. Me-Maw would get up from the table and go over to the sink, wet a paper towel, and then turn to come back to table, chanting and laughing "I'm coming to get you." At the same time Pop-Pop was getting Lucy Ann to cover her face with her hands and both would chant "Oh No, Me-Maw is coming, Me-Maw is coming." A comedy scene for sure, but effective in cleaning up the little princess. And yes, Me-Maw and Pop-Pop did what every other set of parents, and grandparents do, they placed a large plastic sheet under the little princess's food bunker to catch the lightning-fast projectiles from her lofty perch.

Language development in a child might be the most interesting part of nurturing and watching the growth in this little bundle of joy. The initial wailing, crying and even sometime laughter is the only means Lucy Ann had in communicating her inner being with her unfamiliar environment. It must be very frightening moments for these little ones to want something and not explicitly being able to convey their thoughts. Nevertheless, the progression of language development begins, and

the child starts to say words, mostly after, of course, prompting from the parents and grandparents. Mommy, Daddy and then even Me-Maw and Pop- Pop, warmth in our heart's springs eternal. This experience of watching, and hopefully contributing to, the child's communication skills progress is a wonderful time in all parents and grandparents' lives.
To think this child, with its initial tabula rasa, begins to integrate with its surrounding environment is a magnificent wonder to watch, and yes it takes patience and effort to support this, but the inner warmth and joy of being part of this growth is a thing of beauty and a life- long memory. More words develop, milk, play, eat, arm, leg, nose, eyes, ears,

diaper, poop, socks, shoes, endless to say the least, and the anticipation of a complete sentence always kept you on the edge of your seat.

Lucy Ann's first sentence, of course a pleasant surprise but nonetheless humorous, was the result of tender teasing of Lucy Ann when she would knock something over, or just make a mess of things, and Me-Maw and Pop- Pop would jokingly say "It's not me." Well, one day after Lucy Ann had made one of her messes, turned to Me-Maw and Pop-Pop and proudly proclaimed "It's not me." Yes, children do listen and mimic their parents and grandparents, so be careful with these creative wonders. A humorous moment for sure.

Getting the relational aspects of our language also brought humorous moments to the progression of Lucy Ann's communication skills. When Lucy Ann wanted Me-Maw or Pop-Pop to hold her, Lucy Ann would come to Me-Maw and Pop-Pop and stretch out her hands. Me-Maw and Pop-Pop would always say to her "Do you want us to hold you?" Well, after a while, when Lucy Ann wanted Me-Maw or Pop-Pop to hold her, she would come over to Me-Maw or Pop-Pop, stretch out her hands and then say, "Hold You." Yes, this took a while to get right but it was fun doing so. It is such an immense joy and wonderment to be able to experience and participate in Lucy Ann's development, it is like watching the spring flowers rise from the earth in their annual birthing, grow stronger each day with nurturing, watering, and fertilizing, and then to anticipate and enjoy their blossoms. And yes, Lucy Ann's blossoming will span yearly spring occurrences, and yes, Me-Maw and Pop-Pop consider this a blessing from above, that they have the means, health, and time to participate, in what could be a life-long blossoming.

And the crawl and those first steps. Hazardous and fearful times for Me- Maw and Pop-Pop, no surprise here. The unfolding of the intricate mechanics of the human body right before your eyes, producing anticipated movements of arms, legs, and fingers, with glorious wonderment on Me-Maw and Pop-Pop's part. Lucy Ann would start out crawling in an unusual fashion, using mostly her arms to push herself in reverse, rather than using her legs to go forward. A confusing maneuver, from Me-Maw and Pop-Pop's point of view, but effective for Lucy Ann in getting to where she was interested in going. If only one could see within that creative little mind as how they perceive things and solve the basic problems confronting them in their new world.

Nonetheless Lucy Ann progressed, of course using her self-determined and unorthodox method of crawling, to being able to go forward with gusto and confidence.

Now, more trouble for Me-Maw and Pop-Pop, more obstacles in the little princess's path to worry about, and then of course the initial reaching efforts by those little fingers to pull herself up and try to become a vertical creature like everyone else. And then the moment of gleeful anticipation and, some trepidation, Lucy Ann stands up and attempts her first steps. Excitement abounds throughout every inch of our bodies, souls, and minds. Endless days of holding Lucy Ann up while she explores her new mobility mechanism, with unbridled enthusiasm and fearless abandonment of any vision of impending doom, and some boom-booms, and was unnerving for Me-Maw and Pop-Pop during those joyful but at times anxious moments. Sharp edges, outer corners of walls, tables to pull over, books to pull from bookshelves, endless potential tragedies in the minds of Me-Maw and Pop-Pop, but obstacles that held no fear for the determined Lucy Ann. How does the child survive all this as they grow, is it the love and care of parents and grandparents, or just the grace of God, surely a wonderment? To participate in this growth is the most important aspect of grandparents, a true blessing in our lives, and Me-Maw and Pop-Pop are grateful that they have the time, and means, to participate in the growth of Lucy Ann. Participating in this growth is a rewarding experience and the elixir that one needs in their lives.

And those days in the parks and outside activities, an unending list of things to do with the little princess. It is fascinating to watch the digestion, by these little creatures, of the unfolding world around them. Larger creatures all around them, sliding doors, revolving doors, cars and trucks, birds and squirrels, an endless sequence of new experiences saturating that child's developing mind. Always done with a little reluctance at first, but always followed by an interest of absorbing more of their unfamiliar environment. It is a magnificent design, this developing brain with its capacity to absorb such unlimited new experiences, and a true testament to a superior being in our universe. The guidance for Lucy Ann during this growth requires attentive and loving parents, and Lucy Ann was fortunate to have such parents. It seems essential to healthy development in all children's lives that they experience this caring and nurturing throughout their early lives, from their parents or single parent. Support from a Me-Maw or Pop-Pop can be helpful also. It was always a joy walking Lucy Ann to the park, watching her take in all the new experiences in her life, different dogs, birds and squirrels, varieties of flowers and plants, cars and trucks whizzing by, crossing areas and of course Lucy Ann's mental GPS recording of where the Ice Cream stand was located.

These walks always initiated a multitude of questions and answers, some that of course taxed the knowledge of Me-Maw and Pop-Pop. Always good bantering with Lucy Ann. And then the playground in the park was our chosen destination on these excursions with Lucy Ann. The playground was a challenge to Lucy Ann at first, watching her gauge the risk and dangers of certain apparatus in the park, the flying swings, the long swirling slides, the climbing devices, and the rotating rides. It took a while, but Lucy Ann started to enjoy all these new experiences. The long swirling slides were a particularly daunting experience, not only for Lucy Ann, but Pop-Pop also.

When Lucy Ann and Pop-Pop would pass the slides, Pop-Pop would always ask if Lucy Ann would like to go down the long swirling slides. Lucy Ann would initially indicate that she did not want to do that, but after a little while, Lucy Ann would take Pop-Pop's hand and declare that they were going to go down the slide together. Pop-Pop may have gotten more than he bargained for on that one. It was certainly a challenge to contort an aging body and go down that slide with Lucy Ann, although a memory Pop-Pop will always cherish. And like reading books to Lucy Ann, it meant doing the effort over and over. The love of this child can certainly be taxing, mentally and physically, but a love that is everlasting.

And those stops at the ice cream stand on the way back from the park, sheer joy on Lucy Ann's face with those eyes of hers lighting up like the brightest stars in the heavens. Pop-Pop would always tease Lucy Ann about the flavor she would get: "Pistachio" for you Lucy Ann? Oh no Pop-Pop, Lucy Ann would reply, Vanilla or Chocolate is the best, Pistachio is not good. Pop-Pop would persist with his support of Pistachio to no avail, as Lucy Ann held her ground with her choices. So, Pop-Pop would get a cone of vanilla or chocolate, cunningly denying Lucy Ann's request for a scoop of both at times. One scoop is always a mess, two scoops are a complete disaster. Pop-Pop would tease Lucy Ann about getting a few licks of the cone for Me-Maw and Pop-Pop. Oh no Pop-Pop, this is only for Lucy Ann. That is not fair Pop-Pop would say, only to hear Lucy Ann reply, "It is Fair, only for Lucy Ann." This sort of bantering would go on for a while, but eventually Lucy Ann would yield a lick or two. It is comical, and a little messy too, watching this child develop exotic techniques for consuming this cone, all the while having it drip on her hands and clothes. A few napkins, of course, and complete attention on the part of Me-Maw and Pop-Pop for this event. The interesting part, a stretch of our imagination, is watching Lucy Ann start to eat the cone from the bottom up. I am not sure what is going on in the minds of these little ones when they do that, but it must be genetic code embedded from the earliest days of human development, since it appears a universal technique for children.

Then the clean-up begins with more napkins and Me-Maw going into her facial clean-up routine with creative pantomime and tons of laughter. Me- Maw getting Lucy Ann to laugh at these times exudes an element of co- operation from Lucy Ann that is a relief and heartwarming to the soul, to say the least. An effort on the part of Me- Maw and Pop-Pop on these ice-cream excursions but mitigated for sure by that expression of sheer joy on Lucy Ann's face. Lovely moments entrenched in our memory banks.

Then there is that moment when this adventurous child, our Lucy Ann, discovers the smart phones of her parents and grandparents and all others that come within her grasp, wow, the strength of those little hands as they wrestle the phone from you without much notice, and of course before you can articulate the grave dangers of such a little one spending too much time with such electronic devices, not much parental hypocrisy here. New rules of engagement are proclaimed from that moment on, time limits established, rules of polite pleading by the child are discussed, and yes, abandoned by the child, and the hiding of our phones from Lucy Ann is crucial for her safe development, preventing "smart phone" brain deterioration in the child of course, not that this happens in adults, for sure. It is amazing to watch this young mind, without any previous training, or even knowing what the device is meant to do, manipulate the buttons to achieve self-satisfaction with exploring photos, causing new panels to pop-up, and of course randomly turning on the flashlight.

Occasionally, Lucy Ann will creatively, to say the least, put the smart phone into a mode of operation, with her Houdini button movements, that none of us ever knew existed in the smart phone.

Always an interesting task to get you smart phone back to ground zero after the magic of the little fingers have been at play. Well, through mystical ancestral oversite from the heavens above, the little angel eventually agreed to a time limit rule of sorts cleverly suggested by her parents, and I have to say, Lucy Ann has embraced this with a non-tantrum modus operandi. These moments when you achieve an element of co-operation with this developing child, after hours of bantering, rulemaking, rule-breaking, seem to generate a warmth and peacefulness within oneself, and obliterate all the struggles up to that point in time. Blessings such as this are the salvation of grandparents, and yes, even an expansion of the wonderful imagination unfolding in that little child's mind.

Ah, that developing world of the young child, fraught with cuts and bruises, accidents galore, stumbles here and there, and yes, joyful moments too, is wonderfully magical as it is complex.

Parents, and Grandparents too, are constantly imposing new rules and restrictions on this developing child and the child's reaction to these impositions on the child's view of how they see interacting with their unfolding world, is of course trying to adults at times, but interesting to watch their creative and rebellious techniques in posturing their opposition to adult rule. "You should have your shoes and socks on," Oh no, no shoes and socks for Lucy

Ann, a definitive voice for sure. Pop-Pop and Me-Maw have started to call Lucy Ann "Nature Girl" for her insistence on bare footedness. And then there are the anatomy debates with this inventive mind, "that's your left foot," Oh no, that is my right foot, rebellious bantering at its best.

Then there are Lucy Ann's more devilish moments. Lucy Ann developed a stealth like move, whenever bagels and smoked salmon were served, by quietly approaching Me-Maw, who is cradling her bagel and smoked salmon topping unaware of this stealth creature, and quickly snatching the smoked salmon from Me-Maw's bagel and moving away from Me-Maw with a tender smirk on her face. And then there is Lucy Ann's hard to contain giddiness as she wanders about the room and pulls the bookmarks out of the books Me-Maw or Pop-Pop are reading. An apparent pleasure in that child's life for whatever reason one can imagine. Of course, the "It's not fair/It is fair" bantering goes on for a while between Pop-Pop and Lucy Ann, resulting in zero long term improvement in this behavior. Being involved with the growth of a child, on all levels, parents, grandparents, aunts, and uncles, can be exhausting at times, but there are those tender moments that will carry the day for all involved.

No better use of time can one expend during one's life.

There is a sense of beauty and inner fulfillment as one, and this is surely a gift, just the grace of God, actively nurtures, and participates in the growth of a child. The magnificence of that experience can be as blinding as the sun and all the stars in the heavens. It is far greater than watching the growth of those spring and summer blossoms that are the results of our timely endeavors, far greater than watching the growth of villages, cities, towns, and nations, and even far greater than watching the growth, hopefully, of our retirement accounts. Yes, far greater than all of those since they are dependent on the growth and nurturing of our children, and yes, all of them not just our own.

The sense of excellence, and an inner sense of well-being, and yes, a sense of spirituality, will only come when all of us, parents, grandparents, aunts, and uncles, actively and lovingly participate in the nurturing and growth of, not only our own, but of all the children that are blessing this world that they live in. It is important to realize that being able to do this requires a certain level of stability in our lives, not that everyone must be a millionaire, maybe in today's jargon a billionaire, but that next week cannot be allowed to project a lack of rent or mortgage payments, or lack of feeding or clothing, or lack of daycare or pre-K, or lack of health care, no it cannot and should not have any of these projections for families, or individuals.

Healthy and developing children are the soul and catalyst for civilization advancing at its best, and civilization must give its undivided attention to its children. All societies, globally and locally, should concentrate on ensuring the stability of the individual and families within their domains, and yes, America will hopefully take the lead in this effort.

Sustainable infrastructure programs, Pre-K and Day-Care, Affordable health care, Vocational and Academic education are the essentials, not mere choices for the well-off, for advancing civilization to its maximal, and its most spiritual, progression that this world has yet seen. Personal accountability and the drive for personal development is very much a part of this process and should be the DNA of civilization's progression. For civilization to realize its full potential, civilization must provide the foundation for nurturing and growing these human characteristics.

Americans need to ensure that our policies and programs support the nurturing and growth of our children, our most valuable assets for sure. And yes, there is a cost to all of this, but the cost of not doing this is far greater, orders of magnitude so, in terms of broken families, drug abuse, crime, expensive incarceration, mental health, and more costly, missing that next Einstein because society failed to provide the foundation.

So, this basic, and empowering, concept, *"Every Child is Everyone's Child,"* is something America, if there is an element of decency, and yes, a spirituality in its core values, and by all societies and countries also, must ingest and take this concept to heart for realizing what may be the greatest growth civilization has ever seen. The effort to embrace this concept is not so daunting as it first appears, but it does require all of us to fully understand that societies, and civilization itself, cannot reach its unlimited potential, without the stability, and growth, of its individuals, and more importantly, that of its families, and yes, it means of all of them.

To believe that the human existence can progress by only thinking of oneself is fraught with such calamities, crime, drugs, mental instability, income inequalities, and only adds up to wasted lives and a cancerous erosion of civilization's lifeblood. It is ludicrous to think that there are large corporations, with billions of dollars in cash reserves, paying zero taxes each year. Let us support corporations with a fair and equitable tax rate, but there should be a minimum tax regardless of any corporate situation.

It is imperative that humanity change its modus operandi, that of self-indulgence, winning at any cost, and yes that of pure greed, to one of giving back a little more than one takes in life. At the end of our lives that daunting question will haunt us, "Have we helped another along the way?" The answer may bring peace and tranquility to our end or that of remorse and anxiety, images that may not be so evident along the way. Leveling the playing field is essential to maximizing the human existence, and it should encompass competitiveness, accountability, individual responsibility, and yes, all these things, and requires all to participate in the game. It is important that societies provide the foundation for individuals and families to compete, and contribute to, civilization's progression, but this foundation must provide inherent stability to ensure the progression can reach its full potential.

Investments in sustainable Infrastructure programs, Pre-K schooling, healthcare, are essential components of providing for that stability in individual and family lives. The sustainable Infrastructure programs are a "no-brainer" since they provide the means for paying for the other essentials. Infrastructure programs put people to work at all levels of the economic scale, they then pay taxes and are not on the government dole, they spend money in their communities, go to restaurants, do home improvements, and so the original investment in infrastructure grows. Businesses that supply materials to support the infrastructure programs grow, they hire more people, and they pay more taxes. The infrastructure programs even provide corporations with a more efficient environment to grow in.

The simple, but ethical and yes spiritually invigorating concept, *"Every Child Is Everyone's Child,"* is a challenge to our society, and the world at large, but it is one that our social, and yes, political, genes must ingest. To not do so only allows the cancerous elements of self-indulgence and personal greed to erode civilization's true potential.

America must take the lead in this effort and ensure that individuals and families have a reasonable chance at a stable existence, allowing them to participate and contribute, in a positive, and yes, spiritual way, to our developing world. It is not evil to want to accumulate wealth, and yes, this is a healthy endeavor for all, but when the accumulation of wealth blinds us to the human condition around us, then, yes, our moral compass drifts from "true north."

Is it not enough that mankind has created a society with such income inequality, such massive incarcerations at enormous and wasteful costs, such rampant drug use and proliferation, such mediocrity in areas of education and infant mortality, such growth in homelessness and mental illness, and such fervor for winning at any cost, a Trumpian fervor that has eroded our democracy and American values and borders on outright communist infiltration, to not give support to this concept of *"Every Child is Everyone's Child,"* And yes, it needs to be part of our American DNA from this point on, a massive NASA like program that put us on the moon, and yes, the NASA program was expensive, but the benefits of that program still ripple through our society even today.

America is a great country. Me-Maw and Pop-Pop are blessed to have been born and live in this country. America possesses enormous potential economically, politically, and morally in advancing civilization, not just for America but the entire world. America's potential decreases with self-indulgence and personal greed, and yes, that winning at any cost. This needs to change for the betterment of all. And for the Evangelicals and Pro-Life people, supporting life just at the moment of birth instead of supporting and nurturing that life from that moment of existence, and supporting single issue candidates that erode the basic foundation of individual and family stability instead of candidates that overall support the foundation for the stability of individual and family lives, this concept, "Every Child is Everyone's Child," may be the solution to eliminating, or reducing to near zero, those abortions that you spend enormous energies in preventing with very dismal results. Pious hypocrisy is not going to eliminate abortions but supporting policies that build the foundations for nurturing our children may well do that, and in the process build a better and more spiritual society for all, not just a select few.

America blessed, ever so by the Grace of God our country believes, with enormous potential, but realizing America's potential, requires that all families, and individuals, need a foundation of stability in their lives for that growth to happen. Let us all be competitive, be responsible and accountable, and yes, let us accumulate wealth to the best of our abilities, but none of this should blind us to the human conditions around us. Self- indulgence, pure greed, and winning at all costs, are eroding America's true potential, and may God forbid, may bring down this great and unique experiment in the world theatre. America must drive its moral compass to "true north" for the sake of all, not just preserving life for the few.

Me-Maw and Pop-Pop have been overjoyed with this gift, this wonderful granddaughter. Me-Maw and Pop-Pop blessed with the ability, and means, to help with the nurturing and growth of this wonderful creature, are enjoying this delightful adventure. It has been a joy to witness, and be involved with, the unfolding realization of this child's view of its expanding, and challenging, world, much different from that cozy and protective womb from which it came.

Parenting, and grandparenting, are essential elements for advancing our human condition, and the best means of civilization realizing its full potential.

Me-Maw and Pop-Pop have been blessed with parents that were caring and nurturing during our childhood days and have provided us with the values that have helped us parenting our own children, and yes, helped with being grandparents, and maybe in all of this one can always do a better job, but it is most, and only, important that one try their best at doing it. And, yes, there are examples of individuals that can parent and grandparent without a level of stability in their lives, but they are the exception, and may God continue to bless their efforts.

America has the potential to provide the foundation for the economic stability to support good parenting, and grandparenting, for all, not just a few.

America's belief in a God-driven universe requires it to take the lead in providing this stability for individuals and families. Turning a blind eye to the human condition around us, does not appear to be a tenet of any God-driven religion. Americans need to embrace with great energy, that simple, magical, and yes, spiritual, concept of *"Every Child is Everyone's Child,"* it could be American's best companion throughout our lives and may be that of civilization, also.

Infrastructure Programs, Pre-K, Day- Care, Health Care and a "Level Playing Field," with justice for all, may be a good start. And for the Supreme Court Justices, when ruling on the issues of the day, the Supreme Court Justices need reminding, that creating things in your own image and likeness, is the domain of the Supreme Being, not the Supreme Court.

Let us not forget that during World War II, America supported high quality Day- Care centers throughout the country to support the Patriotic, and heroic, woman running our manufacturing plants while raising their families. What say, America gives efforts like that a restart?

Acknowledgements: Thanks to Me- Maw, Daughter Katie, and good friends Julie and John for their helpful review comments.

www.ingramcontent.com/pod-product-compliance
Lightning Source LLC
LaVergne TN
LVHW011858060526
838200LV00054B/4403